MAN'S INHUMANITIES

GENOCIDE

By Thom Winckelmann

ERICKSON PRESS

Yankton, South Dakota

For more information, contact:
Erickson Press
329 Broadway
PO Box 33
Yankton, SD 57078

Or you can visit our Web site at **www.ericksonpress.com**

Content Consultant:
Professor Mark Bernstein
Joyce and Edward E. Brewer Chair in Applied Ethics
Philosophy Department, Purdue University

Editor: Amy Van Zee
Copy Editor: Paula Lewis
Design and Production: Becky Daum

Library of Congress Cataloging-in-Publication Data
Winckelmann, Thom.
  Genocide / by Thom Winckelmann.
     p. cm. — (Man's inhumanities)
  Includes bibliographical references and index.
  ISBN 978-1-60217-975-2 (alk. paper)
1. Genocide—Juvenile literature. I. Title. II. Series.

  HV6322.7.W56 2009
  364.15'1—dc22

                                        2008034805

CONTENTS

UNDERSTANDING GENOCIDE

News about the genocide crisis in the Darfur region of Sudan, Africa, may be confusing. Perhaps this is because the word *genocide* is most often linked to the Holocaust under Nazi ruler Adolf Hitler. Many people think that no similar event has happened. They agree that the issue is important. Yet, they do not know it is a current problem.

Some may have heard the word used to describe events that took place in Iraq under fallen dictator Saddam Hussein. An example would be his use of chemical weapons against the Kurds. The Kurds are a minority population that lives in the northern part of Iraq. The term *genocide* is also used to describe the African slave trade. Sometimes it describes the treatment of the indigenous peoples of the Americas. The word is usually used to describe displacement, enslavement, and mass murder.

The Sudanese Liberation Army in North Darfur

In the process of learning about genocide, there may be more questions than answers. What exactly is genocide? How widespread is this problem? Does genocide still occur? Why is it important to learn about genocide?

Chapter 1

DEFINING THE PROBLEM

The word *genocide* was coined by Raphael Lemkin in 1944. The term combines the Greek *genos*, meaning "race," with the Latin *cide*, for "murder."[1] Lemkin created the term for use in his book *Axis Rule in Occupied Europe*. He needed a way to describe the Nazis' slaughter of European Jews. He needed to distinguish the killing of Jews from the mass killings the Nazis inflicted upon others. A word for this situation did not yet exist.

After World War II and the Holocaust had ended, the newly formed United Nations (UN) drew up its Convention on Genocide. Its authors built on the word Lemkin had created. They carefully defined it. They provided conditions to be met and criteria for use in determining if an event is truly genocide.

Lemkin's term and the UN convention made it easier to determine if a humanitarian crisis is

Witnessing Oppression

Raphael Lemkin was born in 1900 and grew up in Poland. He experienced anti-Semitism. Anti-Semitism is hatred or prejudice against Jewish people. He also witnessed some of the events of World War I on the Eastern Front. During this time, he learned of the Armenian genocide. As an adult, he studied other cases of inhumanity. He began working to find ways to protect people from oppression. At the same time, the Nazis came to power in nearby Germany. During World War II, he worked in the United States. He later helped the prosecutors in the War Crimes Tribunal in Nuremberg. Afterward, he worked to ensure that the newly formed UN would put into practice legal protections for victims of genocide.

genocide. However, some argue that the definition is too specific. They worry that the UN will spend too much time debating whether a crisis meets the criteria for genocide. In that time, more people would become victims. Others worry that mass murder might take place without a UN response if the situation did

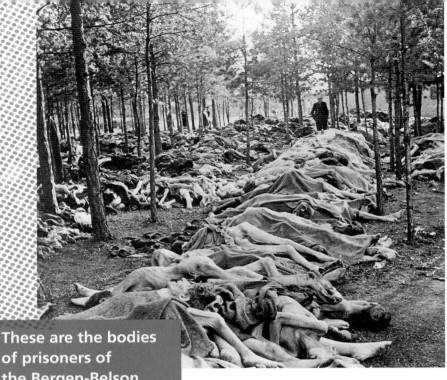

These are the bodies of prisoners of the Bergen-Belson concentration camp in Germany. The photo was taken in 1945 after British troops liberated the camp.

not fit the UN's definition for genocide. Critics argue that the narrow definition used by the UN is not as effective as it could be.

How Widespread Is This Problem?

Many people have the idea that no event of genocide has occurred since 1945. Many also believe that history gives few examples of genocide apart from the Holocaust. But genocide also occurred earlier in the twentieth century. It happened in places such as the former Union of Soviet Socialist Republics (USSR) and the former Ottoman Empire. Genocide existed

How the United Nations Defines Genocide

Article II of the Convention on Genocide provides the legal definition of genocide:

"In the present Convention, genocide means any of the following acts committed with intent to destroy, in whole or in part, a national, ethnical, racial or religious group, as such:

(a) Killing members of the group;

(b) Causing serious bodily or mental harm to members of the group;

(c) Deliberately inflicting on the group conditions of life calculated to bring about its physical destruction in whole or in part;

(d) Imposing measures intended to prevent births within the group;

(e) Forcibly transferring children of the group to another group."[2]

in Africa, Asia, and the Middle East. The Holocaust is perhaps the most well-known example. But it is certainly not the only twentieth-century example of genocide.

A century of genocides

In international law, genocide is the crime of destroying, or committing conspiracy to destroy a national, ethnic, racial, or religious group.

Examples of genocide since 1900

YEAR	LOCATION	ESTIMATED DEATHS
1930s	Soviet Union, Ukraine	6-7 million
1933-'45	Europe	6.0
1975-'79	Cambodia	1.5-2.0
1915	Turkey/Ottoman Empire	1.0
1994	Rwanda	0.8
2003-present	Darfur, Sudan	0.1-0.4
1992-'95	Bosnia-Herzegovina, Serbia, Croatia	0.2
1988	Iraq	0.1-0.2

SOURCE: The World Almanac   AP

Genocides since 1900

Humankind made a lot of progress during the nineteenth century. It was perhaps more progress than in any other 100-year period. By 1895, the countries of Europe had evolved into modern nation-states. The advances of the Industrial Revolution built upon one another. They yielded new economic growth. Improvements in communication and transportation allowed the widespread movement of people, goods, and information. Making food no longer required as much labor. By the end of the nineteenth century, the steamship and the telegraph had become common. Widespread automobile and aircraft travel lay just beyond the horizon.

However, 500,000 or more Armenians died during the 1890s. This was a precursor to the Armenian genocide. The Boer Wars of the 1890s brought death—and the world's first concentration camps—to South Africa. Concentration camps are places where groups of people are kept as prisoners. The Bolshevik Revolution in 1917 and the early years of communism in the Soviet Union brought suffering and death. World War I and World War II

British troops march in Jamestown, South Africa, during the Second Boer War.

were global conflicts. Nearly 100 million people died in these wars.

By 1944, millions of people had been murdered in China, in the Pacific Islands, in the Soviet Union, and in Nazi-controlled Europe. These mass murders took place within a period of less than ten years. Japan, Russia, Georgia (Caucasus Mountains), Mongolia, Germany, Poland, and Ukraine all carried out the killings. Their victims were Chinese, Americans, Germans, Jews, Catholics, and Buddhists. Some victims belonged to ethnic groups marked for death by the killers. Some died on gallows, others on electrified fences. Some killers favored well-organized, high-tech killing methods. Others worked their victims to death or starved them.

Does Genocide Still Take Place?

In the early twenty-first century, genocide still exists. Since the mid-1980s, Sudan has been plagued by civil war. Sudan is a large country in northeastern Africa. It became an independent nation in 1956. However, there were many differences between the leaders in the north and in the south. This fighting between the north and the south has resulted in years of political unrest. It has caused many economic changes. The region has also experienced droughts throughout the past 20 years. These droughts have harmed crops and

Hundreds of thousands of people have been displaced as a result of the crisis in Sudan.

caused massive hunger. Diseases have spread throughout many parts of the country.

In early 2003, another conflict arose in the Darfur region of Sudan. The Darfur region is on the western side of Sudan. Its citizens have been oppressed by a brutal regime. There has been a great deal of conflict over the land and who has rights to claim it. Since 2003, the government has targeted citizens of the Darfur region. Civilians have been attacked. Millions have lost their homes. Hundreds of thousands have fled to neighboring countries. Hundreds of thousands have lost their lives. There have been attempts at peace between the government and the rebel groups. Some groups have cooperated, and some have not. The situation is still tense.

Citizens of other nations also suffer. China, North Korea, Iran, Afghanistan, and Cuba are just examples. Despite much progress, mankind still has the urge to oppress certain groups.

Why Is It Important to Learn About Genocide?

A study of the Holocaust alone ignores other cases of genocide and mass murder. This means nearly 300 million victims from the twentieth century will be forgotten and the survivors will not be remembered. Can citizens of every nation learn to value every human life? The deaths of millions in genocides other than the Holocaust cannot be ignored.

Simon Wiesenthal survived the Nazi concentration camps. He dealt with this issue when he addressed an audience at a synagogue in Manhattan.

Simon Wiesenthal

Simon Wiesenthal was a Holocaust survivor. He spent the rest of his life writing and speaking about the Holocaust. He led the hunt for its murderers. "When history looks back," Wiesenthal explained, "I want people to know the Nazis weren't able to kill millions of people and get away with it."[3] He helped in the capture of more than 1,000 Nazi war criminals.

He said, "Twenty-one nations were with me in the camps. Eleven million died. We must remember the five million non-Jews, including a large percentage of Europe's gypsies. . . . It is not enough only to look back at the Holocaust. We must concern ourselves with the genocides of the future as well as the past. The question is, who will be the Jews next time?"[4]

Chapter 2

THE ARMENIAN GENOCIDE

*A*rmenia has rarely enjoyed independence. Its people were the first to make Christianity their official religion as a nation-state. Armenia has had an unstable history. Throughout this time Armenians have remained religious. Armenia fell first under Greek rule in the 300s BCE. In time, Armenia became part of the Roman Empire. Armenia then fell to the Ottomans in the seventh century CE. In 1991, Armenia gained its independence from the Soviet Union.

The Armenians have lived under different levels of oppression. Life for Armenians became more difficult as time passed. By the nineteenth century, their numbers fell. Much of their surviving population spread across the world in a diaspora. They fled murder and famine in their homeland.

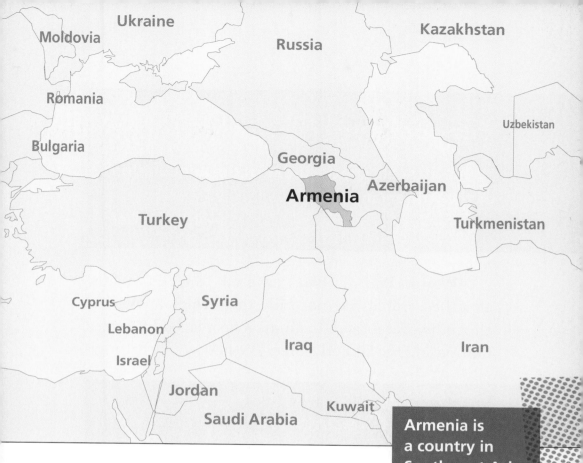

Armenia is a country in Southwest Asia.

There was little tolerance for religious minorities such as Christians in the late nineteenth century Ottoman Empire. It was then that the first of a series of massacres occurred. As many as 500,000 Armenians perished in the mid-1890s under Abdul-Hamid II. Twenty years later, the Armenian genocide took place. The genocide happened under the regime known as the "Young Turks." The Turkish government killed as many as 2 million Armenians. This was the first genocide of the twentieth century. Most were killed between 1914 and 1918 during World War I.

World War I had covered the Ottomans' atrocities. But it did not hide the Armenians' crisis altogether. Reports of the massacres reached Western Europe and the United States. The news came through print media and political and military personnel. German and U.S. embassy staff made reports to their home governments. However, no serious effort at intervention on behalf of the Armenians was made.

During the war years, the *New York Times* ran numerous stories on the events in Armenia. It provided graphic detail and left no doubt as to what the Turks were doing. Readers of these stories were made aware of the mass murders happening around the globe.

News of the massacres also reached the United States and

This image shows bodies of dead Armenians after a massacre. Author Henry Morgenthau wrote that scenes like this were common in the summer of 1915.

Henry Morgenthau served as ambassador to the Ottoman Empire during the time of the mass murders of the Armenians.

other nations through the informal reports of immigrants. Author Peter Morton Coan interviewed immigrants who came to the United States through Ellis Island. Many who arrived in New York between 1914 and 1945 had fled during World War I or World War II. Many fled the violence committed by groups in Nazi Germany and the Ottoman Empire.

Newspaper Headlines

1,500,000 ARMENIANS STARVE
Relief Committee Asks Aid for Victims of
Turkish Decrees.
New York Times, September 5, 1915

**ANSWER MORGENTHAU BY HANGING
ARMENIANS**
He Protests Against the War of Extermination
Now in Progress.
New York Times, September 16, 1915

WE CAN DO NOTHING FURTHER
View of State Department as to Action
Regarding Armenia.
New York Times, October 16, 1915

POPE MAY MAKE NEW PLEA TO KAISER
T.P. O'Connor Hears He Will Be Asked to Take
Action to Save the Armenians...
New York Times, December 9, 1915

James Karavolas immigrated to the United States from Greece in 1915. He told Coan "the Turks were coming. All the people that got killed, their bodies were piled up on the sidewalk. It was horrible. Blood all over."[3]

The Armenian massacre

Between 1908 and 1913 the "Young Turks" party seized power from Sultan Abdul Hamid. The leaders, Pashas Talaat, Enver and Cemal, were in power during the slaughter of the Armenians. By Turkish estimates, hundreds of thousands were killed. Many were suspected of collaboration with Turkey's Russian enemies. During the years 1913-1923, Armenians claimed that as many as 1.5 million died.

Talaat

Enver   **Cemal**

The Young Turks

1915	1916	1917	1918	1919	1920	1921	1922	1923

April 24: 800 Armenian leaders, writers and intellectuals were arrested and many killed or deported

June 1 Thousands of Armenians serving in the Turkish military were disarmed and sent to labor camps; many died

Oct. 30: Armistice ended war between Allies and Turkey; hostilities remained

Jan. 8: Sultan Mahmed VI ordered criminal prosecution of "Young Turks" in their absence; most of them fled the country

February: Turks regained power in Cilicia when French forces withdrew from post-war occupation; thousands of Armenians were killed

July 24: Treaty of Lausanne recognized the new Republic of Turkey

SOURCE: Documents from German State Archives

William J. Castello • AP

A timeline of the Armenian massacre

Sera Tartunian's family survived the massacre of Armenians during World War I. But her family had to flee Turkish oppression and violence after the war. Her father was killed in her presence. She fled with her mother and sister. On the way to take refuge with U.S. missionaries in a nearby town, Tartunian witnessed a horrible scene at the local orphanage: "Here's an army truck, and do you know what they were putting into the army truck? The dead bodies of the orphans. The bodies were being thrown out the windows into a truck. These were Armenian orphans."[4] Coan recorded many stories such as these.

Coan's work was done mostly near the end of his subjects' lives. His work saves important accounts and provides evidence of atrocities that few acknowledge. International apathy regarding Turkey and its victims continued into the late twentieth century. Other events had priority in the international community and in the media. The Turkish government continues to deny that the genocide took place at all.

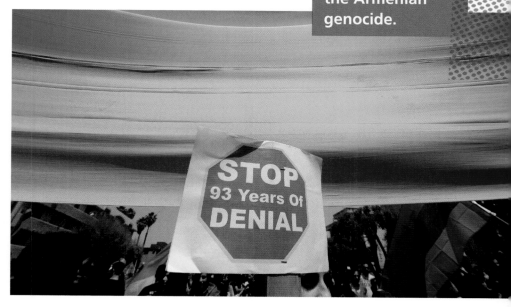

Protesters gather in Los Angeles in 2008 to mark the ninety-third anniversary of the Armenian genocide.

STOP 93 Years Of DENIAL

Chapter 3

THE HOLOCAUST

*T*heodor Herzl tried to help European Jews establish a homeland in Israel. By June of 1895, he had made little progress. Herzl was the founder of the Zionist movement. The Zionist movement grew in response to discrimination against Jewish people. The leaders of the Zionist movement wanted to establish a homeland for Jewish people.

Assimilated Jews enjoyed the benefits of Western Europe's culture and its economy. But in the 1930s, Adolf Hitler came to power in Germany. The state of Israel finally came into being in 1948. By that time, it was too late for nearly half of Europe's Jews.

The Holocaust raises important questions. How much was known about the Holocaust during the war? Was there prewar evidence that an event such as the Holocaust might happen? By the time of the Holocaust, mass killings had already occurred in

Turkey, the Soviet Union, and in parts of China that were controlled by the Japanese. Should world leaders have taken the Nazi regime's anti-Jewish speech and actions more seriously? Could people in Nazi Germany and its occupied territories have done anything to prevent the Holocaust? What can be done to ensure that the future will not include another holocaust and additional victims?

There were warning signs in events that took place long before Hitler became Chancellor of Germany in January 1933. Hitler's *Mein Kampf* was published in 1925. Hatred for the Jews was evident in the book. The hatred was also seen in the anti-Semitic speeches of the Nazis. Hitler did not have the opportunity to act until he came to power. Official acts against Jews began gradually. To people who held anti-Jewish feelings or stood to gain in some way, these laws may not have seemed alarming.

These Polish Jews are being deported by German soldiers.

But looking back, the laws show a disturbing hatred toward Jewish people.

In April 1933, the Nazis began encouraging a boycott of Jewish-owned businesses. Then the "Laws for the Reestablishment of the Civil Service" kept Jews from getting important federal and municipal jobs. The "Laws for the Protection of German Blood and the German Honor" prohibited "mixed" marriages as well as extramarital affairs between Jews and non-Jews.[2] These laws were commonly known as the Nuremberg Laws. Why didn't German citizens speak out against these unfair actions toward Jews?

Hitler's early years in power were times of great change and growing prosperity for Germany. The majority of citizens benefited. Jews and other minorities suffered. Hitler employed Germans on massive public works projects. He began a huge program to build up weapons. This action violated the Versailles Treaty that ended World War I. He also increased the ranks of the military far beyond the limits set by the treaty. Foreign investors returned to Germany. They helped fund Hitler's plans. These funds strengthened Germany's economy. Ordinary Germans were content to let the Nazis take care of government matters. The citizens went on with their daily lives. They did not seem to mind how the

Speaking Out

"First they came for the Communists, but I was not a Communist so I did not speak out. Then they came for the Socialists and the Trade Unionists, but I was neither, so I did not speak out. Then they came for the Jews, but I was not a Jew so I did not speak out. And when they came for me, there was no one left to speak out for me."[3]

—*Pastor Martin Niemöller*

These children were liberated from the Auschwitz concentration camp by Soviet forces in January, 1945.

Nazis dealt with the mentally ill, political dissidents, communists, Jehovah's Witnesses, and Jews.

Die Endlösung (The Final Solution)

War became a reality with Germany's invasion of Poland in September 1939. Jews could not leave Germany legally. War also showed signs of what European Jews would face under the Nazis. First Polish, then Czechoslovakian, Jews were resettled in ghettos. The Nazi war machine rolled across one country after another. Jews from other parts of occupied Europe were also cut off in major ghetto communities.

These ghettos made the Holocaust possible. Large groups of Jews were gathered in ghettos. Once this was done, it was easy to kill many at once. Also, the communities may have given a false feeling of safety to some Jews. In the ghettos, they settled into lives that became familiar. European Jews had survived being forced into ghettos in the Middle Ages.

Die Vernichtungslager (The Extermination Camps)

The transition from ghettos to concentration camps began slowly. Germans had grown used to seeing their Jewish neighbors disappear to the concentration camps. Once the war began, the number and size of the camps increased. The list of offenses that resulted in imprisonment also grew. Some of these camps also served as work camps. The expanding German military needed labor to support its growth. Finally, the Nazis envisioned camps of another kind. They used the camps to deal with people whose only crime was their identity.

Hitler was victorious in Western Europe. He was at a standoff in the air war with Britain. He soon turned his attention to Eastern Europe. Hitler dreamed of one day gaining "living space" for the German people. He imagined an empire stretching from western France all the way across the Soviet Union.

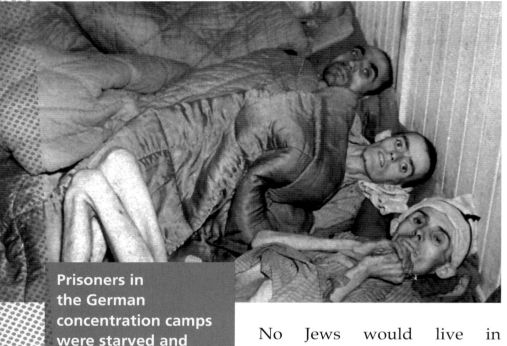

Prisoners in the German concentration camps were starved and overworked.

No Jews would live in this empire. In addition to conquering nations, this plan also required a solution to what Hitler called "the Jewish problem."

To make Europe what they called *Judenfrei*, or "free of Jews," the Nazis needed a way to kill nearly 12 million people. German forces set out toward the Soviet Union on June 22, 1942. The phrase "Final Solution" first appeared in correspondence between S.S. General Reinhard Heydrich and other members of the Nazi leadership. New facilities were built in Poland. There was a labor camp on the outskirts of a Polish community once known as *Oświęcim*.

The Germans called it Auschwitz. Near this camp, a second camp named Birkenau opened. The new camp was not another labor camp, but a death camp. Heydrich sent task forces in charge of executing Jews to the camp. He also sent members of the German army. Later they used special convoy routes and railroads to transport people to the death camps. These camps, Treblinka, Sobibor, Chelmno, Majdanek, and Belzec, in addition

There are many stories of the terrible treatment of prisoners at Auschwitz. Some prisoners were even used in horrific experiments.

Baltic
Sea

Stutthof

Neuengamme

Ravensbrück
Sachsenhausen-
Oranienburg
Bergen-
Belsen
Berlin
Chelmno
Warsaw
Sobibor

Elbe
Oder
Dora-Mittelbau
Gross-Rosen
POLAND
Majadenek
Buchenwald
Belzec
Theresienstadt
Auschwitz-
Birkenau
GERMANY
Prague
CZECH REP.
Flossenbürg

Mauthausen-
Gusen
Natzweiler-
Struthof
Danube
Dachau
Vienna

FRANCE
AUSTRIA

SLOVENIA
San Sabba
CROATIA
Jasenovac

Treblinka

Vistula

Rhine

This map shows
the locations of
the major death
and concentration
camps in Central
and Eastern Europe.

to Auschwitz-Birkenau, became
the primary killing centers.

The Germans could not spare
enough ammunition to shoot all
of the European Jews. Carbon
monoxide poisoning proved slow and unreliable.
German chemical company I.G. Farben soon solved
these problems. Zyklon-B gas proved remarkably
successful. Camp staff poured the gas into rooftop

pipes atop shower buildings. The inmates went into the showers for "decontamination." The shower room doors were locked, and the victims were gassed to death. The gas chambers were successful, but there was another problem. The Germans then had to deal with thousands of corpses.

Another German firm designed and constructed huge

Some men and women who suffered in the concentration camps lived to tell their stories.

furnaces. Inmates who had been selected for labor placed the bodies of the victims into the furnaces. The camps worked at a high level of efficiency. By the time Hitler died, as many as 13 million people had perished in the camps. This included nearly 6 million Jews. In fewer than five years, Hitler had murdered more than half the Jews in Europe.

Chapter 4

THE CAMBODIAN GENOCIDE

One of the worst mass killings of the twentieth century took place in Cambodia. In April 1975, the armies of communist North Vietnam approached the outskirts of Saigon. Saigon was South Vietnam's capital. Communist forces of the Khmer Rouge advanced toward the Cambodian capital of Phnom Penh. A man called Pol Pot led the forces. The Khmer Rouge was his regime. Pol Pot had pledged to transform Cambodia into a paradise for farmers and other working-class people. The Khmer Rouge emptied Cambodia's cities of people. They wanted to change Cambodia into a country of farmers. The Khmer Rouge wanted to create a mainly agrarian society. To do this, they believed they had to cut their country's ties to other nations and to modern times.

Pol Pot became the prime minister of Cambodia in 1976. But his interest in politics had begun long before he took power. Pol Pot grew up in financial abundance. He received a higher education in France. Many privileged members of society had these opportunities. He did poorly as an electrical engineering student. Politics captured his interest instead. While in France, he met members of the Communist Party. Pol Pot remembered what he had read in the works of Karl Marx and Mao Zedong.

Marx was a nineteenth-century political thinker. Zedong was a Chinese political leader.

Pol Pot returned to Cambodia in 1954. When he returned, he began to seek a way to apply what he had learned. With help from communist forces in North Vietnam, he got his chance in 1970. Neighboring Vietnam was at war. This helped pave his way. He was also aided by a strong communist movement in Laos and a weak government in Cambodia. The spread of communism was a very large world issue. In less than four years, Pol Pot would become one of history's biggest mass murderers.

His idea was to start anew at the "Year Zero." The government would force many citizens to be reeducated in this new way of life. However, the Khmer Rouge declared many citizens to be beyond hope. Perhaps these people had worked for Western businesses or governments. Perhaps they spoke foreign languages. Some had earned college degrees or technical certifications. They may have been too old,

Tragedy

"The death of one man is a tragedy; The death of a million is a statistic."[1]

—Attributed to Joseph Stalin

Pol Pot was the leader of the Khmer Rouge. He wanted Cambodia to return to an agrarian society.

sick, or weak to perform farm work. The Khmer Rouge saw these people as fit for death.

There were many changes under Pol Pot's leadership. His government made religion illegal. They also closed schools. Children were instead sent to serve in the military. The government seized control of businesses. Banks and other businesses that used international trade were not allowed to interact with foreigners. Many Cambodians who lived in the city were forced to work on farms. Also, those who owned land were forced to give it over to the government.

Pol Pot forced many of the Cambodian people into rural labor camps. Thousands of people were murdered at these "killing fields." For the executions, the Khmer

Under Pol Pot's regime, Cambodians died of starvation and overwork. Many were murdered.

After Pol Pot's regime fell, hundreds of corpses were found in the "killing fields."

Rouge did not want to waste ammunition. Like the Nazis, they found other ways to kill their victims. Men and women were murdered using axes, knives, and sometimes even bamboo sticks. Many were tortured before they were killed. Some starved to death. Today, these killing fields contain mass graves. The bones of those who died are still visible.

Over the years, hundreds of thousands fled their homes in terror. Many trekked through the jungles to Thailand only to suffer in refugee camps. Others risked their lives at sea, becoming "boat people." How many of them drowned or died of exposure is unknown. Others survived the Khmer Rouge only to die when Vietnam invaded Cambodia in 1978. Thousands more were maimed or killed by land mines and other explosives left behind by war.

The Aftermath

The Cambodian genocide is an unusual example of genocide. It represents a case where Cambodians were killing Cambodians. Tourists visit the country now to see the temples and the killing fields. Workers still repair the damages brought by decades of warfare. Land mines still litter the countryside. Cambodia is still in the process of recovery.

Pol Pot died in 1998 shortly before his seventy-third birthday. Unlike the leaders of Nazi Germany, he never faced justice for his crimes against humanity. Pol Pot suffered neither the punishment of his

Reign of Terror

country's legal system nor the wrath of an angry citizenry. His crimes were terrible. He caused the deaths of as many as one third of the citizens he was supposed to lead and protect. At the time of his death, he was under house arrest by his own Khmer Rouge for ordering the death of a fellow party member.

In 2007 a tribunal, or committee, was formed in Cambodia. The tribunal was much like the one responsible for bringing the perpetrators of the Holocaust to justice. But unlike the Nuremberg trial, this one came into being nearly 30 years too late. Many of the perpetrators, including Pol Pot, were already dead. Others were in hiding. Survivors had left the country, succumbed to their injuries, or died of old age.

The United States had pledged to come to the aid of the Cambodian government and that of South

Authorities say that the Khmer Rouge's victims were tied together with rope before being executed.

Vietnam. But things had changed. In 1974, President Richard Nixon resigned from office. President Gerald Ford had little power in dealing with the House and Senate. Finally, Congress voted to end funding for military and economic aid to Southeast Asia. The United States had spent nearly 20 years trying to limit the growth of communism. Aid to forces struggling against communist uprisings in other parts of the world, including Africa, ended with awful results.

Cambodians are still dealing with the after-effects of the genocide.

The consequences did not end with the Ford administration. They carried through to President Jimmy Carter. By the time Carter left office, as many as 2.4 million people had died in Cambodia from the Khmer Rouge. The end of the Cold War a decade later, along with the collapse of the Soviet Union, should have brought relief. In instances such as these, it is difficult to understand how the rest of the world can watch and do nothing while one country is suffering greatly.

Chapter 5

GLOBAL BYSTANDERS

*T*he failure to act quickly can have tragic costs. Historically, genocides have provided grim lessons for bystanders to crimes against humanity.

The United Nations (UN) has many peace-keeping duties. The UN seeks to maintain good relations between nations. It also pledges to stand up for human rights and individual freedoms. But the UN has also taken on the responsibility of identifying and stopping genocide. Individuals such as Simon Wiesenthal worked for the capture of escaped war criminals. They have made it difficult for such individuals to flee their pasts.

Tens of millions of people have died in mass killings around the globe since the Holocaust and since the creation of the UN. As World War II ended and the Cold War began, priorities changed.

Many nations focused on competition for political, military, and economic power. Perhaps the international community lost sight of more important goals. The UN made much progress in other areas. But the UN often failed to perform its most vital function: the saving of lives. Communist regimes were allowed to grow until they became impossible to defeat quickly or through military force alone. This helped the regimes become the worst of the twentieth century's mass murderers. China and the Union of Soviet Socialist Republics (USSR) became responsible for as many as 100 million deaths. Most of these happened during the regimes of Mao Zedong in China and Joseph Stalin in the USSR.

The Communist Party

"Probably 61,911,000 people, 54,769,000 of them citizens, have been murdered by the Communist Party—the government—of the Soviet Union. This is about 178 people for each letter, comma, period, digit, and other character in this book."[1]

—*R. J. Rummel,* Lethal Politics: Soviet Genocide and Mass Murder since 1917

Mao Zedong helped make China a communist nation.

From 1958 to 1969, approximately 75 million people died in the People's Republic of China. This was under the regime of Mao Zedong. The UN did not act. But this was not the only oppressive government. A cruel regime was allowed to hold power in North Korea beyond the century's end. UN peacekeepers arrived in Cambodia more than ten years after the last of the Khmer Rouge's victims died.

Looking Back

"We did not act quickly enough after the killing began. We should not have allowed the refugee camps to become safe havens for the killers. We did not immediately call these crimes by their rightful name: genocide."[2]

—Bill Clinton on the Rwandan genocide

At one time, Rwanda was one of Africa's most densely populated nations. However, in the mid-1990s, as many as 1 million people became genocide victims. Millions more became refugees. Tensions between the tribes of the Hutu and the Tutsi built for months. This crisis did not build in secret. Travelers, businesspersons, missionaries, humanitarian and human rights workers, and the members of various nongovernmental organizations

Humanity for All

"There are no humans more human than others."[3]

—Romeo Dallaire

Niger
Chad
Nigeria
Sudan
Eritrea
Dijbouti
Ethiopia
Central African Republic
Cameroon
Equatorial Guinea
Somalia
Gabon Congo
Uganda Kenya
Rwanda
Dem. Rep. of Congo
Burundi
Tanzania
Angola
Malawi
Zambia
Mozambique
Zimbabwe
Namibia
Botswana
Madagascar

Central Africa

witnessed events in Rwanda. They began telling the UN, Western governments, and the media about the situation in Rwanda at least a year before the mass killings began.

Once the frenzy of killing began, 75 percent of Tutsis in Rwanda lost their lives. The Hutu killed more than 700,000 people in just six weeks. Because tensions built over such a long period, the UN had ample time to plan and carry out peacekeeping operations.

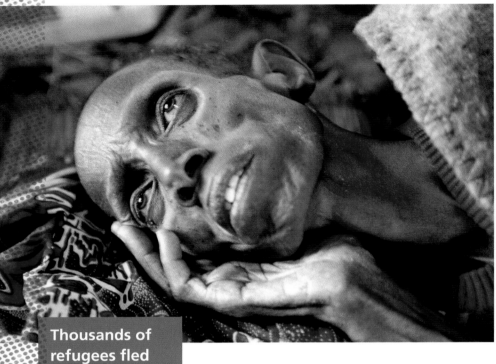

Thousands of refugees fled the Rwandan crisis. Many were starving and sick.

Even with a small peacekeeping force in Rwanda during the genocide, though, such operations never took place.

The Clinton administration and UN leaders debated whether the mass killings constituted genocide. During this time, the murders in Rwanda continued. Secretary of State Madeleine Albright was concerned about whether getting involved in Rwanda would advance U.S. interests. President Bill Clinton decided to keep U.S. forces out of Rwanda. The small UN

Global Apathy

"The international community didn't [care about] Rwandans because Rwanda was a country of no strategic importance."[4]

—*Romeo Dallaire*

peacekeeping force in Rwanda under the command of Canadian General Romeo Dallaire was prepared to help. However, UN leaders ordered him to "take no action" and finally withdrew the force to safety. This left the Tutsis to defend themselves. General Dallaire remarked, "We could have stopped it."[5] Looking back, the regret over inaction makes the tragedy even more painful.

World Awareness

Americans are drawn to any story of individual struggle. People are genuinely saddened, in most cases, by individual tragedy. There is little reason to believe that others around the world do not share these views, no matter how different the cultures may be in other ways. Nations across the world continue to ignore cases of genocide and mass murder. This is not entirely the fault of the citizens. Societies have other priorities. If students and citizens are to be

Tanzania received many of the Rwandan refugees.

aware of world events and make good decisions about their leaders and governments, they need the facts. The same is true in order to gain a complete understanding of genocide and mass murder.

The U.S. Department of State reports serious human rights concerns in dozens of nations. These include abuses against women and children, singling out of religious and ethnic minorities, repression of political dissidents, and trafficking in human beings. Groups such as Human Rights Watch and Genocide Watch warn of current or imminent genocide or mass killings in African countries such as Sudan, Ivory Coast (Cote d'Ivoire), Burundi, Congo, Zimbabwe, and the Asian country of Chechnya. The news media does not always make great efforts to bring this information to citizens in general or to students in particular.

The United States, British, and Australian forces have secured large areas of Iraq. As they do so,

Bulldozers were used to shovel the bodies of Rwandans into mass graves.

international journalists gain access to increasingly alarming textual, physical, and eyewitness evidence. This evidence shows shocking violence committed in Iraq during the toppled regime of Saddam Hussein. Few newspapers or television networks report their findings.

However, a democratic form of government depends on educated, well-informed citizens. Accurate information is needed to make reasoned decisions and to make our views known to our elected officials. Upon learning about the extent to which genocide has taken place, and still does take place, some may wonder why such important issues have been ignored.

Genocide's history is long, as is its list of victims. The memory of the people must be honored. Learning is one way to achieve this. Gaining the will to act is another. Only then can genocide become a problem of the past.

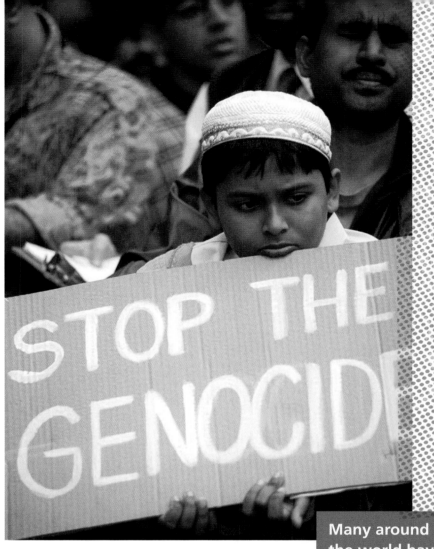

Many around the world have united to raise awareness of genocide so that it can be stopped before it starts.

Glossary

Anti-Semitism
Hostility to or prejudice against Jews.

Assimilate
Absorb ideas, values, and ways of life to integrate into a society.

Atrocity
An act that is wicked, violent, or cruel.

Boycott
Protest by refusing to buy goods or services.

Communism
A form of government where all land, houses, factories, etc., belong to the government or community and profits are shared by all.

Diaspora
Distribution of people, usually involuntarily, from their original homeland.

Dissident
Person who is against a government or its policies.

Ghetto
A part of a city where minorities, historically Jews, live in isolation by law.

Indigenous
Native to a particular place.

Intervention
Interference by a country or countries in another country's activities.

Perpetrator
Person or group responsible for a harmful or illegal act.

Refugees
People forced to leave their homes because of war.

Regime
A government that rules during a certain period of time.

More Information

Books

Coan, Peter Morton. *Ellis Island Interview: In Their Own Words*. New York: Checkmark Books, 1997.

Pastore, Clare. *Journey to America: Chantrea Conway's Story: A Voyage from Cambodia in 1975*. Berkeley, CA: Berkeley Publishing Group, 2001.

Silverman, Robin Landew. *A Bosnian Family: Journey Between Two Worlds*. Minneapolis, MN: Lerner Publications, 1997.

Xavier, John. *Darfur: African Genocide*. New York: Rosen Publishing Group, 2007.

Web Sites

Human Rights Watch (www.hrw.org). Human Rights Watch is committed to justice, freedom, and the protection of human rights around the world.

United States Holocaust Memorial Museum (www.ushmm. org). The United States Holocaust Memorial Museum seeks to maintain human dignity and stop genocide.

Yale Cambodian Genocide Project (www.yale.edu/cgp). This Yale program has studied the Cambodian genocide since 1994. The Web site offers statistics and other information about the tragedy in Cambodia.

Notes

Chapter 1. Defining the Problem

1. "Raphael Lemkin." *United States Holocaust Memorial Committee on Conscience.* 5 May 2008 <http://www.ushmm.org/conscience/history/lemkin>.
2. "Convention on the Prevention and Punishment of the Crime of Genocide." *United Nations Commissioner for Human Rights.* 5 May 2008 <http://www.unhchr.ch/html/menu3/b/p_genoci.htm>.
3. "Simon Wiesenthal." *Simon Wiesenthal Center.* 2 May 2008 <http://www.wiesenthal.com/site/pp.asp?c=fwLYKnN8LzH&b=242614>.
4. Richard Korn. "Origins of the Institute for the Study of Genocide." 23 June 2008 <http://sonic.net/~doretk/Issues/96-12%20DEC/institutetotudygenocide.html>.

Chapter 2. The Armenian Genocide

1. "Adolf Hitler." *Armenian National Institute.* 19 May 2008 <http://www.armenian-genocide.org/Hitler.html>.
2. R. J. Rummel. *Statistics of Democide, Genocide, and Mass Murder since 1900.* Charlottesville, VA: Center for National Security Law, School of Law, University of Virginia, 1997. 36.
3. Peter Morton Coan. *Ellis Island Interview: In Their Own Words.* New York: Checkmark Books, 1997. 278.
4. Ibid. 396.

Chapter 3. The Holocaust

1. "Herzl Speaks His Mind on Issues, Events and Men." *World Zionist Organization*. 17 May 2008 <http://www.wzo.org.il/en/resources/view.asp?id=1631>.
2. "The Nuremberg Laws." *Jewish Virtual Library*. 15 Apr. 2008 <http://www.us-israel.org/jsource/Holocaust/nurlaws.html>.
3. "Martin Niemoeller." *Jewish Virtual Library*. 19 May 2008 <http://www.jewishvirtuallibrary.org/jsource/biography/niemoeller.html>.
4. Press Release. *Armenian National Committee of America*. 21 May 2008 <http://www.anca.org/press_releases/press_releases.php?prid=1>.

Chapter 4. The Cambodian Genocide

1. Karen Lawrence. "International Dimensions of Genocide." *London School of Economics and Political Science*. 1996. 19 May 2008 <http://www.veritnet.com/karen/genocide.html>.
2. Dith Pran, comp. "Children of Cambodia's Killing Fields." *New York Times Books*. 15 May 2008 <http://www.nytimes.com/books/first/p/pran-cambodia.html>.

Chapter 5. Global Bystanders

1. R. J. Rummel. "Lethal Politics: Soviet Genocide and Mass Murder since 1917." *Transaction Publishers*, 1990. 15 May 2008 <http://www.hawaii.edu/powerkills/NOTE4.HTM>.
2. "100 Days of Slaughter: A Chronology of U.S./U.N. Actions." *PBS/Frontline*. 15 May 2008 <http://www.pbs.org/wgbh/pages/frontline/shows/evil/etc/slaughter.html>.
3. "A Good Man in Hell: General Romeo Dallaire and the Rwanda Genocide." 12 June 2002. *United States Holocaust Memorial Museum*. 27 June 2008 <http://www.ushmm.org/conscience/analysis/details.php?content=2002-06-12>.
4. Ibid.
5. Robert M. Press. *The New Africa: Dispatches from a Changing Continent*. Gainesville, FL: University Press of Florida, 1999.

Index

About the Author

Thom Winckelmann is a freelance editor, writer, and writing consultant living in Central Florida, where he also teaches college-level humanities and history. Currently at work on his doctoral dissertation toward a PhD in history, he specializes in Holocaust and genocide studies.

Photo Credits